I0521806

SPIRIT OF LOVE

SPIRIT OF LOVE

LYNNE BERGHORN

AUCTOREM
HOUSE

Auctorem House
276 5th Ave, Ste 704-2591
New York, NY 10001
www.auctoremhouse.com
Phone: 1 888-332-7718

© 2025 Lynne Berghorn. All rights reserved.

No part of this book may be reproduced, stored in a retrieval system, or transmitted by any means without the written permission of the author.

Published by Auctorem House: 12/02/2025

ISBN: 978-1-968059-28-6(sc)
ISBN: 978-1-968059-29-3(e)

Any people depicted in stock imagery provided by iStock are models, and such images are being used for illustrative purposes only.

Certain stock imagery © iStock.

Because of the dynamic nature of the Internet, any web addresses or links contained in this book may have changed since publication and may no longer be valid. The views expressed in this work are solely those of the author and do not necessarily reflect the views of the publisher, and the publisher hereby disclaims any responsibility for them.

Table of Contents

Dedicated to my Husband

Barry

With Love and Gratitude

With Love and Appreciation

To Forrest, my Son, and His lovely Wife, Jenna

And their Daughter, Blake

For the Spirit in each of us

For the child in each of us

Spirit of Love

My heart sings
As I look at nature
All around me.

The breeze sends
A sweet caress
Telling me I'm being watched.

Cooling winds remind me
It is relieving me
Of the hot sun.

The sunset is red
With passion
By those of us who witness.

The night stars
Enchanting us to make love
Shining with your embrace.

With love I write poetry
Observing the star-filled sky
Passioned with love and romance.

Dancing with God

I danced with God today.
He's a wonderful dancer!
Hands touching,
moving, swaying,
we didn't miss a beat!
As we danced,
I prayed.
My hands tingled,
And more than leading me,
God was loving me.
Together we did
A dance of praise.

Speaking to God

I'll talk to You,
And then I'll listen
And hope to hear Your voice.

I'll sing to You,
And then I'll listen
And hope to hear Your voice.

I'll look to man,
And then I'll listen
And then I'll hear Your voice.

I'll look to man,
And then I'll see
Your sweetness in his face.

It's You in him
And You in me
The way we can relate.

Magic Circle

Thoughts and secrets,
Boo-boos and troubles,
Laughter and sneezes,
Even hugs and squeezes,

Memories and warm feelings
Your gifts to me,
Notes and drawings
Treasures I'll always keep.

You've made me feel important
Dear children,
With your kind
And caring ways!

Always remember your magic
Listening and talking
Sending love
All around the circle.

I'll never forget you!

Your Mirror

Look at me
And see
Your love
In bloom.
I do so well
With kind words.
You see
My precious gift
Of trust,
And hold me dear.
Fragile I'm not,
Because as I open
Our beauty clear,
STRENGTH
Will come in our creation.
TRUTH,
The water that makes us grow.
Your best thoughts and words reflect,
I'm willing to be Your mirror.

Awaken

The white blanket of snow lay quiet
And undisturbed as far as I could see.
"Come and lay by me," it invites.
A soft blanket on which to cuddle.
The lightness and beauty calls to me
To sleep like a doe under a moving sky.
Forgetting the cold, I wrap myself
In the arms of snow.
Dreaming of peace, the heavens open up
And bring me in.
From there I gaze down,
Sleeping with God's love on his face.
"Awaken,
it's time for you to run and play."

Dreams

The pretty flute in the mist of the playful harmony
Stirred fantasies of woodland creatures,
Twitterpated and playing in a soft summer breeze.
An announcement blown by the horns,
Heralded the arrival of the Prince.
A hush fell in the forest,
And across a grassy meadow,
Rode the Prince on his black steed.
Regally he sat, but his heart was lonely,
His quest for a bride unfulfilled.
"Where is she, the one I'll love
She who makes me happy?"
Were his days to be spent alone
Performing God's gifts in his creation?
The tempo quickened and signaled a change.
Playful fingers danced across the keys of the piano,
And imagination provided a woman of his dreams.
Sweet melodic harmony with the strings
Set a romance in play.
The glory of nature,
The fantasy of the woodland creatures,
The love of the Prince and mystery lady,
Provided by a composer unknown to me,
Mystic, impressionistic dreams of a winter's day.

The Day I Was Juliet

You painted my walls
With a feather
Burnt amber forever.
I was Juliet that day
Reading Longfellow
On the carpet stairs.
Your smile
Warmed my back,
You stopped
And said, "Beautiful,"
Just the way
I felt.
You allowed me
My romantic self
As you worked.

Sunflowers

Sunflowers dance
In a diamond-sparkled pond.
The sun's warm breath
Nurturing their growth.
Enhanced by the other,
The picture prettier
As two.

The Dancers

One day a pretty girl
Who had an awful limp,
Was playing in her garden.
After doing a dance,
She sat awhile and wondered
As she so often did,
How lovely she could be
If she could dance without a limp.
She was a lovely child
Gentle and kind,
But had a will that could not bend.
Many people said she was a stubborn child,
And so when she looked in the mirror,
She wasn't sure who was there.

Unaware that he had been watching for several days,
She saw a young man in her garden.
It was odd seeing his face,
Such an air of familiarity.
It was like seeing her male face.
He was a dancer and reflected to her
Another image of herself.
He extended his hand,
And together they began to move around the garden.
Slowly at first, and then faster and faster…
Until smooth… She danced
As she had never danced before!
He blew a kiss and said goodbye.

Dream she often did of that magic day.
She had changed so!
Now she knew who she was
A dancer!
Together they had shown the other a new mirror.

Little Dandelion

Pretty little dandelion
Yellow gold.
Whoever said you were
a weed?
I always saw you
As a flower,
And picked you
For my Mother
After school.

Merci, Mon Adieu

Heavenly Father
Brightest star in the sky,
Thank You for courage
And taking me so far.
Thank You for the hope,
And the promise of tomorrow.
Help me stop the shakes
As I quake at the changes.
Help me continue walking
On Your path of loving health.
Thank You for the charity
And vision of Your truth.
Thank You for the charity
And kindness of new fiends.
Help me be Your instrument,
And speak with Love and Truth.

God's Song

Flowers all comely
Whisper a stroke
Gently sing
A hymn to Me.

Work a thunder
Lightning strike
Heaven awaits
Your slumber.

Lullaby, sweet angel
Don't you cry
No burden too great
To carry.

The time is past
To doubt, My lass
Press on
Don't tarry.

In just a while
The bells will ring.
You'll hear My song
Joy it brings.

Lost Sheep

We must do the best we can to peel labels,
To expect the best from one another,
To Love,
To Trust,
To Forgive,
The only name to call one another is
Brother or Sister.
We must extend ourselves
To find the Lost Sheep.
We must offer friendship
In spite of past mistakes.
The fear of falling under the influence
Of the Lost Sheep,
Must be less than the knowledge
That love can bring him back to the fold.
We all have a mission,
And that mission is to do God's work.
The interpretations people cast on your work,
Cannot alter your path.
With prayer, your course will become clear.
God will show you the way you can best do His will.
There are no "Dregs in Society,"
There are just people
Struggling, some lost, some faltering, some clear.
For those of you
Who today are clear,
Give a hand to those of us who are stumbling.
With your loving hand
Comes the opportunity for us to heal,
And extend our hand to someone else.

San Diego Animal Park

Lilies, ice plant, orchids everywhere,
And colored trees, purple, orange, and blue,
Carpeted the land besides the walks.
Monkeys, leopards, lions, and zebras
Baby rhinos delighted us.
Going around in a monorail.
Animals free to roam
Vast expanse of dirt and trees
For their leisure and their play
Doing what they please.
Taught us to throw our cares away.
In their natural environment
These animals were a happy lot.
It really was a pleasure to see
The San Diego Animal Park.

All in a Time

All in a time
Slowly evolving,
Don't rush an answer.

All in a time
As we're ready
To hear and move on.

All in a time
As we know
The picture clears.

All in time
With prayer
The spirit heals.

All in a time
We'll approach
the Truth.

All in a time
The light will shine.

The Wizard and Athena

The wizard stood above the pot
Stirring the streaming dark liquid,
While Athena watched from above.
Looking down inside the cauldron,
Lives of people struggled to get out.
Snatched from the streets,
When looking for gold
Tricked by the wizard,
They were thrown into the vat.
This enraged Athena,
The people subject to the power of the wizard.
So to him she did appear.
"Listen now! Give me your ear."
And forthwith she poured into him
The wisdom of her years:
"No one is subject to you or anyone here.
Though they quest for gold,
Their lives are not yours to have.
They must journey on their own path."
And so the wizard and Athena agreed,
And they sprinkled magic stars into the cauldron.
Slowly the steam rose and disappeared.
The liquid cooled and turned a mellow green
And lovely pink, the lives released
To find the beauty in the flowers.

Slipped Away

Murky, foggy, swampy night,
Lights and noise from afar,
The bars in the distance
Stank with liquor and smoke.
By the pier,
She stood in a long coat,
A hood around her face.
Troubled and afraid,
She wished to escape the bawdy crowd.
Unaware of her absence,
They continued to drink and swear.
She longed and wished for a light from a boat.
In the distance, a light appeared,
And the boat came quietly to shore.
Inside the small canoe was a man
She somehow knew.
An instant recognition crossed
Their hearts and face.
Without a word, she got into the boat.
He silently rowed away.
From the dirt, she escaped.
Into the fog, they disappeared.
What happened, we'll never know,
But rescued from degeneration,
She had safely slipped away.

A Sea

Like a sea
The boundaries disappear.
I look at you
And feel it's me.
What does it mean
This eclipse of reality?
A blending
A oneness
Hard to discern.
Our separateness
An experience
That causes doubt.
An entry
Into an unknown realm.
A blending
of you and me
Like a sea.

Choices

You laid her
In bed.

You covered her
In primary colors.

You said,
"Trust me."

Her love apparent
She showed vulnerability.

You extended your hand,
You offered a boat.

Your symbol of transference,
An implied shared journey.

Red, yellow, blue
Trusting you.

She lay in bed
In love.

Touch

Good morning,
Peekaboo
Are you there?

She raised her head from her pillow,
And saw a smiling face
Of her little boy wonder.

A smile lit her face
As she blew a kiss,
And he quietly closed their half-shut door.

She stretched…
Turning her naked body into the warm,
Strong body of her husband sleeping beside her.

She leaned into him
Warm, impressing her limbs
With the strength she gained from him.

His fingers plied gently
Against her skin
Indicating his pleasure.

She felt happy,
A beautiful son, a strong husband,
That this would never change!

She would remember this morning,
And use this memory to quiet the doubts
When they came again.

What could be healthier
Than the love and security
She felt in her family.

One

Quiet my restlessness
Still my anxiousness
Let me feel Your love.
Let me know Your strength
Allow Your entry
Enjoy Your peace.

Answers will come
If I allow You to speak.
Give me the faith.
Allow me to feel Your presence.
Let me feel the confidence
Of Your love.

Conflict

A funny site won't leave my mind.
A picture of conflict I've contrived.
Picture this, if you will,
A kitchen stacked with dirty dishes.
On a stool, in the center,
Sits a girl, prayerful but clad very playful.
A red satin brassiere, black silk panties,
In her hands a rosary.
Rather inappropriate, we're told!
Who is this girl anyway?
A picture of Conflict
I'm told…

Lost

In a fog she wandered,
She had heard his voice softly calling,
But that was long ago.
Which direction should she go?
Puddles and debris littered the way,
Into the smelly mud she would sink,
If carefully she didn't proceed.
Was it possible to exit this maze,
Without the help of her friend?
Totally lost, fighting defeat,
She felt her way through the fog,
But why did he not respond to her cries for help?
Was he lost and alone,
Afraid to show he knew no more than she?
A mist began to fall,
And with it some clarity.
She was the leader, not he.
To find the path was up to her,
He was more lost then she.

Letting Go

To play, to play, to play
How silly not to play!
If you are able
And can dance
Are you afraid
To take a chance?
If music
Is your chosen field
Sonatas, concertos
You should yield
A snicker here
A snicker there
To run and hide
A blanket warm?
Be brave dear friends
At trumpet horn.
Slash that paint
The beauty thrives,
The pen a picture makes.
To play, to play, to play
How silly not to play!

The Puppet

I am your puppet
Jiggle my strings,
I am your clay
Do what you please.

Always, forever
Happy I'll be
As long as you play me,
And pull all of my strings.

I can make music,
I can make dance,
I can bring Joy,
Beauty, Romance.

So please
Be patient and see,
I'll cut the strings
For both you and me.

Inspiration

The dramatic sweep of the artist's brush
Passioned red across the canvas
As Brahms grandly announced
The beginning of his first "Piano Concerto."
Leading into a suspenseful merger of mystery and romance,
The artist dabbed color from his pallet,
To gather strength and imagination
From the gifts of another,
Is a secret artists know well.
As the music softened and hushed,
As if from a great distance
Blues and greens appeared on the canvas
Adding a cooling, receding display.
As the music danced, the colors dotted in a Seurat-type effect.
The lust combined with a soft mystic
Giving the painting a look of contemporary romance.
Guided by the music and directed by his talent,
The artist created a masterpiece for God and man.

Embracing a Wish

I Hold on
For dear life
Listening to
Your heartbeat.

We stand
As one
Clinging not wanting
To let go.

I hear your life
Pass to me.
I stand taller
Because of you.

I dare
Where I only
Dreamed
I could go.

Meeting you
Gave courage,
Making dreams
Come true.

Your presence
Is sweetness.
Your silence
A void to fill.

Sunrise

Clouds of charcoal gray
Created mystery in the sky.
Streaks of scarlet pink
Rested against the morning horizon

Puddles filled the playing fields
and the Little Miami flooded over.
Beacons of light lined
The Beechmont Levee.

He painted this beautiful painting
And I gratefully ask
That I may pass it on to you
Reminiscent of a Turner past.

The Docent Class

The buzz of gossip and chatter
Stimulated by art and matter,
Lights bright in the auditorium
Ladies standing in their own euphoria.

Observing again, forming an impression
My pen jots thoughts, notes, descriptions
To scribble a picture with imagination and fun,
Words will tell what I have done.

DaVinci, Signorelli, Botticelli
Famous painters make believe
To look, to love, a story they tell
Beautiful paintings cast a spell.

To experience art an emotion for me.
From an artist's brush to my heart you see.
Vicarious experience brought to us all
Dear painters and writers, a wonderful call!

Dogwoods

Pretty dogwoods
White and pink,
Cheering my way to work
Driving through Eden Park,
Spring dancing
Feeling a lark.
Seasons bless beauty with beauty.
Dogwoods, lilies, daffodils
Open your eyes.
Drink in the sights
Spring is here!
Pretty dogwoods
Pink and white.

Strawberries

He was so tall
That morning
As he walked
To the screen door.
Slowly, with purpose
Full of emotion,
Sweetly we made
Breakfast,
And ate strawberries
In the sun.

The Candle

The candle flickers hope
Casting shadows on the bedroom wall.
The subtle scent added sensuality,
And the birds sang in the early hour
Of five o'clock dawn.
The quietness except for nature's song
Allowed thoughts to come,
And praise filled her mind
With the freedom to write.
Not disturbing anyone,
She sat in her bed alone
Composing.
The candle flickers hope.
The aromatic perfume of the candle,
A gift from my dear friend, Meta,
The presence of a soul mate
Touching the paper.
The song of the birds,
The darkness of early dawn,
Not alone, she felt connected
To nature and her friends as she wrote.
Painting a beautiful picture, she smiled,
Turned out the light and watched.
The candle flickers hope.

The Earth's Wrap

The crispy, red dry fingers
Blow along the soft white tresses of the Earth's wrap.
Small fingers blown by the wind,
Playing and entertaining this viewer.
Some fingers still attached to the black barked trees.
The wind chimes sing,
And the fingers struggle to be free,
And play on the white tresses.
Red, White, Black
Wind chime music,
Whoever said,
"A dull gray day."
Surely he must be dead!

A Picture

Dripping wet, the snow melted
As the bright sun smiled.
Upon the glistening cover,
Shadows cast from the trees
Created charcoal gray.
Imprinting the slowly melting fluff
With a picture so beautiful to please.
Lovely melting icicles
Shone brightly in the glow,
Wrapped around the branches
Melting quickly as I speak.
All this I describe,
As an exquisite wrapped present,
A treasure of blessing to find.

New York Underground

Subway signals, dirty talk,
Grasping meanings
She fought and fought.
A look from her perceived,
Cast shadows on their evil deeds.
Survived she did, a little scarred.
They felt ashamed and turned away.
Forevermore their guilt dissuade.

The Cowboy

Across the broad plains
Of the rugged West,
Rides a lone cowboy
Stirring dust in his wake.
Beautifully fit,
Easy riding,
Skilled and relaxed.
His destination
Is not in my observation.
Rugged, gentleman cowboy
Where are you going?

Spirits

It was magic,
The night, the air,
The beautiful dress,
The music and dance.
Tonight was the night
She knew,
She would meet him
Of whom she had dreamt for years.
Tonight she would see his face,
Feel his embrace,
And dance until dawn.
Anticipation and hope
Filled her eyes and heart,
As she scanned the crowd,
Looking for her mystery man.
Many requested a dance,
And around the floor she swirled,
But the magic was not there.
The hour was growing late,
And her sense of hope began to fade.
Into the garden she walked,
Dejected and sad.
Onto the lake, she cast her eyes.
The moon shimmering,
The lights and stars casting diamonds
Upon the glassy, still surface of the water.
Would her dream be fulfilled on earth?
"Excuse me," he said.
"May I stand with you awhile?"
She turned her eyes and saw her other face.
Their spirits met
That glorious, beautiful night.

Dawn

When the sun begins to rise,
Brilliant pinks and purples streak the sky.
I turn my sleepy eyes toward the light,
And thank the Lord with a prayer.
Across the fields the Little Miami flooded,
And looks like a lake.
Lunken's greens puddled sheets of ice.
Our tree painted by Britton,
Different in every season,
But always strong, asymmetrical in design.
It's a beautiful sight upon which to cast my eyes
Each morning at dawn.

Zarabanda

Cronyism in the Arts
Music, poetry, mime
Favorable influences
Better than the political kind.

An Artist's Salon
To share the wealth
Mix in creativity,
A hub, a light giving way.

To strike a chord,
Inspire another,
Listen and encourage
Is a ZARABANDA'S Day

Bodysurf

A sense of relief washed over her
Like the breaking wave of the ocean.
Bracing for the onslaught,
The water rushed
And with success,
She met the wave.
Wonderful, it felt so good!
She was ready for another.
For once she had done it.
It was not so hard.
She had learned to let go.
Now she could roll
In the feisty sea of life.

In God's Hand

Sunbeams, sun wash
Across the dewy
Yellow meadow

Skies paint
After rainfall
A pretty color halo

Balls fall
As children call
In games and fun

The Earth's sons
Run and play
Act and say

Glory be
Across the land
In God's hand

Fleur

Je suis une fleur
rien a peur
hold me Cherie
a tu je donne
the best je fais
tout le monde
respondez
tu est l'on

Earth

I am the EARTH
Vast and strong
Upon this land
Sow your seeds.
Nourish and grow
In time I'll reap
And send your knowledge
Out to sea.

My Tulip Dream

I had a dream eons ago
Of brightly colored tulips
Sunning in a field.
Then a gentle rain began to fall,
A pretty patter on their lovely pedals.
Reds, yellows, oranges, and scarlets,
beckoning your admiration.
"Please don't pick me," they would say,
And shrink from your gasp, if indeed a bouquet
You thought to make.
"Let us be. We're not here for you to have, but just to see.
It's for our Maker we're here, to give glory"
And so it is with us.
Not for our brother or sister are we here,
But to glorify and honor our Father.
And if this is what we do, then yes
Our brothers and sisters will benefit too.
But not for them or for us
Should we do the things we do,
Just for God are we upon this earth.

Searching

I will find solace in Your words.
I will find comfort in Your love.
I will find knowledge in my search for truth.
Sleep will allow the cleansing rains to come,
And tomorrow I awake refreshed and calm
To begin a day of hopeful love.
To speak with similar expression, perhaps
Only with the books on the shelves.
A kindred spirit, mine has passed me by.
Goodbye, Dear Spirit, wherever you go
I'll be grateful for the dreams
I realized in me.

Different Drummers

Captivating, obligating,
Choiceless fate
Magnetic pull
Oh so great!
Take it easy,
Take it slow,
Where we're going
No one knows.
Easy does it
Let's unfold
Lovely flowers
To behold.
Singing hearts
Persistent thoughts
Forward goes
The God blessed march!

Perceptions

Tiptoes, Whispers
Playful Tales
Did she or didn't she?
Sinful wails
Naivete or cunning wits,
Sink or swim
As go the ships,
Questioning madness
Magic lies
Creative skills
A gift from on high.
How it's seen
My beholder knows
It's in my will
He helped fulfill.

The Fox

He was crafty and sly,
Silent but watchful,
Alert to danger,
Mindful to disguise
His motivations.
Growing up on the streets
Had burned his soul.
Mistrust was as persistent
As his quest for love,
But how could both exist
When one canceled the other
Would love conquer this sly fox?
Could he believe that another
Could love him for himself,
And not harbor secret ambitions?
Until he began to open up,
The cagey fox would remain
Elusive, a lonely creature
In a sea of mistrust.

Connections

Twinkling, blinking, flicking lights
Across the earth at night
Airplanes, headlights, trains and stars
All the activity afar.

As we sit in our homes
Quiet and content,
I often wonder what's going on
In the lights of the night.

So many stories, so many lives
Of interest and concern.
Beside a friend, toast a friend
His face maybe that light.

To connect and see
The light in me
And I in you
This bond will take.

And together all across the earth
Twinkling stars we'll make.

My Father

I am Your angel!
I am Your song!
Who but You embraces me?
My steadfast Love!
I'm a child of Heaven
To be taken above.
Never abandoned, never alone
Your promises assure me!
I'll sing You praises
All day long!

Dew, "A Valentine's Sonnet"

Like dew
I want to
Kiss you.
Like one
I want to
hold you.
Your words
Like velvet,
Your touch
I sweetly imagine!
Perhaps a look
From you convey
Your thoughts
Please display!

Napa City Lights

The crowd gathers,
People milling about
Under the scarlet-streaked sky.

The sound of music
Fills the festive air,
California twilight.
Children laughing
Dogs running
In the sunset breeze.
Adults unwinding, relaxing
On a Friday's eve.
City nights on the river,
Celebrate the concert fair.
A community united at Veterans Park.
California twilight,
Napa City nights.

Precious Delivery

Limousines, chauffeurs,
Pink and blue balloons,
An opening? Not a delivery!
A very special delivery!
From Korea to San Francisco
A little bundle of joy!
Via the Children's Home Society
I presented a baby
To happy adopting parents!
They shared their gift with me!

A greeter, an adoption greeter,
The stars shone bright
Around that slice of life!
Walking down the concourse
Holding that sweet infant
Against my breast,
I felt a part of an incredible day!
International Adoption Greeter
Children's Home Society;
A wonderful, exciting memory!

Trust

Having opened myself
To your redeeming love,
Each day dawns with hope,
And anticipation for a journey
Of promise and surprise!

My soul feels quiet
As my eyes take in the many beauties,
And gifts all around me.
The anxiety of change
Subsides as I trust You!

Placing ourselves in Your hands,
Simplifies and improves all things.
When you work through us,
Our lives become fulfilling,
Our sleep more deep!

Tu, My Steadfast Love

Brush me with Tenderness
Sing to me with Wind,
Vision me in Blueness,
Bless me Again!

You dazzle me with Beauty,
You embrace me with Love.
You guide me with Wisdom,
You shower me with Stars!

Father of Mercy,
Father of Grace,
I am Awaiting
Your sweet Embrace!

Trusting You, I surrender,
I reach for Your arms!
God, our Creator,
Our Savior, my Friend!

Hope

Tiny flower of hope
Bloom in my heart and mind.
Extinguish these flames
Of doubt and heartache.
Quiet the shivers of uncertainty
As the future stems doomed with failure.
Strengthen my faith so I might feel peace
With the promise of Your mercy.
Look at me with compassion
As I stretch for Your
Love, Hope, and Comfort.

Inspiration

The dramatic sweep of the artist's brush
emits red across the canvas.
Listening as Brahms grandly announces
his first piano concerto.
The artist is led into a passionate
merger of mystery and harmony.
Dabbing color from his palette,
he imagines a picture
the composer is helping him paint.
As the music softens and whispers,
blues and greens appear on the canvas.
While the music dances, colors are dotted
in Seurat pointillism.
Lust combines with a soft mystique,
giving the painting a feeling:
contemporary romance.
Guided by inspiration,
The artist creates a masterpiece
For God and man.

"Challenges"

I took the river walk today
In the early morning darkness.
The sun yet to rise.
My Shepherd walked beside me.

The river was full.
It ran quickly, quietly
Enhanced by the dim stars,
And boats by the moor.

The wind was quite brisk.
It had been a short walk
To reach this lovely place,
And wash away the tears.

Shall I end my fate,
Challenges of bipolar disease?
My Mother and
Sisters so far away!

My sweet Mom no longer my confidant!
Alzheimer's disease of Dementia
Destroying my Mother
I once knew.

And then I saw
a group of Angels.
I felt them embrace me.
There's more work for you to do!

All will be okay you must trust.
Your Mom will fall asleep.
She'll be in Heaven,
And you will carry on!

The Angels disappeared.
The sun had risen.

I went home,
And went back to sleep.

And God Said, "Yes"

And God said, "Yes!"
And He smiled.
The orange moon glowed
Against the black sky
While balls of light lined the highway
As cars passed by.
Inside they dined aware
Of the blessing they witnessed:
Affirmation in Creation.
Every day, every moment
A gift to be taken.
Looking for an answer?
Observe the world around you.
Signals come
Solicited through prayer.
They're unobserved by the unfaithful,
Understood by those who seek.
Imagined? I think not!
Go with it, the flow of grace
Will never cease.
And God smiled.

Mother's Hands

Small gentle hands
My mother's hands
Warm and tender
Touching me with love.

Softly she takes
My hand in hers.
Silently, she reassures
With a caress.

After a tirade,
After my tears,
My hand in hers
Receives a squeeze.

Mother, dear Mother
With your hands
You show me
How much you care.

Now when my son
Comes to me
I take his hand
With your touch.

Small gentle hands
Over generations pass love.

Sunshine Love

Starfish, sunny, glistening sand
Aqua water
Caribbean tan
Colorful sails
Wet footprints
Secluded caves
Ensure the pleasure
Of newlywed loves.

Hang On

"Hang on just a little longer,
your mommy will soon be here!"
I kneel tenderly, holding
the broken child in the street.
The driver stands back,
appalled by what he'd done!
The warm golden liquid he'd swallowed
to get a glow, had turned to bile;
a poison he now abhors!
One drink too many, one broken child
casts him into stone.
"Please, God, where's the mother?" he implores!
"Let the child get up," he prays.
"Hang on just a little longer,
your mommy will soon be here."

Our Children

We're here to protect, to guide them
along life's troubled way.
They're not ours
They're God's.
It's just with us they stay.

Our children watch us.
Regard your language,
Use modest, gentle actions.
Discipline with kindness,
Never hit a child.

Ugly words cut a life.
It's with love they best can learn.
To begin each day with a grateful prayer,
helps our humor and our patience.
With love our children return home to God.

Hopes and Dreams

Brilliant colors
Subtle hues
Sky's awakening
Sun's adieus

Glimmering moss
Shiny pebbles
Sandy beaches
Lapping waves

Dogs barking
Children shouting
Sounds of music
Soothing, laughing

Each day
Invites anew
Hopes and dreams
That can come true

Discovery

Like a dream she evolves
into the woman she wants to be.
In love, she thrives.
Her role changes like the man she loves.

A kaleidoscope of emotion and color
her appearance and interests turn,
bringing forth new abilities.
With confidence, she lets go.

In love she discovers
a new dimension.
She stretches and grows.
Her's a journey to self-discovery.

Valentine Days

Come and play with me.
Take the day off,
Enjoy the sun, or
Sprinkles in the rain.

We'll go to a park,
See the beauty
In the sky.

We'll rub noses,
Feel the tips of our tongues
With little kisses.

We'll hold hands, ride bikes,
Perhaps, we'll end the day
In a sweat.

Hearts racing,
Out of breath.
Let me spend time with you.

We deserve memories
Of loving, valentine days.

The Wedding

The cathedral is celestial.
Rays of sun stream through the stained glass.
Tall and regal he waits at the altar,
Her prince of a thousand years.

Radiantly, she glides down the aisle.
The long train of lace slows her step;
A dream… A vision…
Perhaps a reverie?

Her love guides her.
His eyes draw her
Closer, closer to his side.
She's his beautiful, enchanted bride.

Reaching the altar,
They stand side by side.
Under the stained-glass window,
Before God and all, they say,

"We are man and wife."

Untitled

As she stretched toward her potential,
she became like crystal,
sharp, fine, but ready to shatter.

Somehow she disallowed
growth from illness to health.
Success terrified her.

Uncertainty caused her to
struggle for control.
She fought the flaw.

Like a violin, she needed a virtuoso.
She must give the bow to the Master.
She would be played with skill.

Worrying would set her back.
With trust and love,
She would hear her music.

Love Letters

Dear Debussy,
Your "Reverie" takes me back
to days of dreams
and sweet imaginings,
pink Mimosa trees,
ballets and romance.
Listening to you
I bravely take a chance.

Satie,
Your "Gymnopédies" rubs my back,
compresses my brow,
soothes my tension,
sleeps me awhile.
With tiptoes and whispers,
gently you tell me
how much you care.

Beethoven,
The "Pastoral Symphony,"
what a playful fantasy!
Beethoven, dear, Beethoven,
You're a master of every mood!

Rose

Rose, rose, rose,
Your prickly thorns ravished my body.
You scarred my legs, my arms.

Your intoxicating fragrance enveloped me.
For just a brief time,
I held you in my hand.

I felt tender, sweet love.
Your soft, red petals
Touched my heart.

For those cherished moments,
My eyes did not see
The scars that you had brought.

Goodbye, Sweet Rose

Goodbye, sweet rose.
Your fragrance fills the air.
You are so near, but the invisible fence
Threatens to shock if too close I walk.

How wretched I feel!
I need the velvet touch of your petals.
Though never in a thousand years,
Would I pick you from the ground!

The challenge is immense
To survive without proximity
To your gentle feel.
Who set up the fence?

My heart and mind cries to be closer
To you, beautiful, living rose.
Independently you grow,
Giving beauty to the world around.

Sweet, lovely rose, you stand alone.

Song and War

The choirs sang
outside my bedroom window.
A litany of neighbor's voices
wished me well.

The Persian Gulf War
tore my mind and heart apart.
Violent scenes of invasion
threatened me.

I could no longer contain my thoughts.
I was a prisoner of unreality.
I submerged myself in the comfort of water,
disengaging from the terrors haunting me.

The warm water enveloped me.
I let my head float.
I focused on my hair,
Like seaweed, it distracted me.

With growing concern,
my husband watched me.
He stayed by my side,
unable to touch me.

Seeking security,
My mind brought forth friends.
A choir of neighbors sang
Outside my bedroom window.

Royal Ascot

Spinning my kaleidoscope
Memories play
Like notes of a tune
Royal Ascot in June.

My dear Audrey
My fair lady
Me like you
It was déjà vu.

Pleasing parasols peek-a-boo,
Floral flocks flirt
Top hats, bowlers
Oh so British morning suits!

A race, a picnic for a queen
Ascot, Windsor, a fashion scene!

Jockeys parade blue and red silks,
We place bets with punter.
Accents, dress, horses, the bets,
Scones, strawberry jam, clotted cream,

Friendly toasts of bubbly champagne,
Oh look—Queen Mother is seen!

With a gracious wave,
Her sweet smile wands our way.
My quill imprints
The sparkle of the day.

My kaleidoscope spins
A romantic play,
An English reverie,
A golden memory

Closeness

Hold me close
Don't let me go!
Guide me Father
By your Word!

I seek your face,
I need your touch.
I praise You God!
Your gifts I take!

Tall Stacks

Like bubbles of champagne
Throngs of smiling people
snap photos of
Tall Stacks "95."

Graceful boats from Mark Twain's age
float on the Ohio River
in a colorful parade.
They bring our past to present day.

Massive floating vessels
with many ribboned tiers
bear regal names:
Delta Queen, *Belle of Louisville*.

On the decks
are crowds of people
waving flags,
red, white, and blue.

Along the Serpentine Wall
young and old watched.
Their mind etch the scene,
Autum red, gold, and green.

In sunshine the river sparkles
Enchanting the people
like diamonds, Cincinnati,
Queen city, it's a proud October day!

The Night Watchman

She felt mortal pain,
But whose was it?
Someone was going to die,
At least she felt that way.

She prowled the house
Looking for the evil that stalked her family.
Everyone was sleeping well.
But she could only rest.

She lived with fear,
And grew smaller and smaller.

Mrs. Reilly's Bird

Several times a day
A little bird visits Mrs. Reilly.
He sits on her window ledge,
rustles his wings today. "Hello."

He's Mrs. Reilly's bird.
A sweet "Hello" sung
several times a day.
All the better because he's free.

Free to fly, free to stay away,
Yet each day he comes,
he sings, "Hello."
Mrs. Reilly's smile welcomes him.

Lying in her bed,
she turns her head.
She says, "He's here."
A little bird, Mrs. Reilly's bird.

Waterfalls

As the sparkling water
cascades over the boulders,
Beautiful waterfalls form.

In the dazzling sunlight
I let my worries and cares
roll off my shoulders.

I see their insignificance
as I look at the beauty,
the awesomeness of nature.

I feel God's caring
loving hand in play.
I have only to ask Him.

And I will never carry
My burdens alone.

Dreams

The pretty flute in the midst of a playful harmony
Stirred fantasies of woodland creatures,
Twitterpated and playing in a soft summer breeze.
An announcement blown by the horns,
Heralded the arrival of the Prince.
A hush fell in the forest,
And across the grassy meadow,
Rode the Prince on his black steed.
Regally he sat, but heart was lonely,
His quest for a bride unfulfilled,
"Where is she, the one I'll love,
She who makes me happy?"
Were his days to be spent alone
Performing his gifts in God's creation?
The tempo quickened and signaled a change.
Playful fingers danced across the keys of a piano,
And imagination provided a woman of his dreams.
Sweet melodic harmony with the strings
Set a romance into play.
The glory of nature,
The fantasy of the woodland creatures,
The love of the Prince and mystery lady,
Provided by a composer unknown to me,
Mystic impressionistic dreams of a writer's day.

Somewhere

Somewhere, someplace
I'll find You!
My heart seeks You
My mind longs for You.
You are my refuge
You are my strength!

Loving You
Will bring joy,
A slice of eternal peace!
You are there with Your staff,
To rescue me
From anxiety!

Somewhere, someplace
I'll find You!

War

If there must be War,
Aim an arrow of Kindness.
If there must be War,
Fill your cannons with Understanding.
If there must be War
Arm yourself with Knowledge.
If there must be War,
Drop bombs of Love.

Jealousy

Jealousy cuts the veins of life.
It seeks to isolate,
and lives with fear.
It is afraid to loose
that which it claims
to love the most.
Jealousy stifles growth,
And starves love.

Stars

Heavenly stars
In a black sky
Twinkling their encouragement.
"Well done," they say.
"You were good this day.
Don't look back,
Look up!
We'll twinkle and show you the way."
Separately they shine,
Casting their glow, not joining another.
Beautiful together, they twinkle under
The full and glorious Moon.

Blue Coral Garden

Spectacular colors moving about:
Iridescent orange
Purple and pink
Yellow and green.
The fins do sing as around the garden
They swim.
Little fish, cardinal fish, surgeon fish, and awesome
Spectacular colors filling our vision.

A Flame of Gold

The fire burned
flickering specks of gold,
igniting the love she felt inside.

The sliding glass doors
Reflected the golden flames.
Outside a glistening blanket of snow,

Created a picture
Only God could paint.
Snug in her bed,

She watched the fire
The gentle, falling snow.
Beside her curled Jack,

Her yellow, sleeping cat.

Thanksgiving

God opened the stalwart Gates,
And sent forth scores of Angels
To protect His children from the greedy.
Commercial side of the Santa Claus season.

Hundreds of shimmering white lights
Beautifully wrapped His Angels
Disguised as glowing trees
That brightly lined Michigan Avenue.

No one suspected the pretty little trees,
Richly decorated for the festive holidays
Were Angelic Guards, sparkling and twinkling
Protecting us from Devil's greed.

On a quiet Thanksgiving eve,
One could stroll the streets and dream,
Imagining with growing wonder
The promise of Christmas Day.

But the day following Thanksgiving
Heralded a new breed of shoppers.
They pushed forward competing
To save a dollar, to get the best buy.

The meandering shoppers felt rushed.
Fantasy was certainly lost.
Little treasures became hard to find.
Creative thoughts were pushed aside.

To the rescuer, Monet took dreamers away.
Not from the crowds, but from the frenzied turmoil,
He brought us to the Art Institute and securely
Wrapped us in lovely scenes of Giverny.

With kindred spirits, we dreamily disengaged.
Monet took us sailing in Argenteuil.

Showed us a sunset over Parliament,
And invited us to his lush, sunset garden.

Merci beaucoup, Claude Monet!
Your vast display of color, mood, and time
Renewed our sagging spirits,
Increased our pleasure of present the day.

As we left his home of art,
Once again the shimmering lights
Encompassed us, God's reminder,
His guardian surround us.

The Monet show, the Chicago Symphony,
Turkey with relatives and friends,
Second City, tea at the Drake,
C'est domage, the end is here.

We basked in friendship and love,
Given a collage of paintings, music, evergreens.
This cornucopia provided poems,
Fantasies, dreams, and memories.

My Sleeping Cat

Music dances across the air,
sunshine brightens the Autumn colors.
On the terrace, the poets infuse
the beauty of the moment, the day.

My lazy, yellow cat
Curls into the chair beside me.
A friendly day, a colorful day,
I feel wrapped in confidence.

Shimmering, green canopies
topping black barked trees
cast shadows
on the sunlit grass.

A lonely picnic table
waiting for four,
shaded by an impressive catalpa tree,
asks to be part of the story.

Poets observe,
watch, listen.
With rhyme, rhythm
they pen the scene.

Jack sleeps,
Soft and curled
Oblivious
To the poet's pen.

This and That

Wine and food
Lots of wine!
He looked at her,
But not quite like that!
He looked at her,
And only saw that and that!
She wanted to know him,
But not yet, like that.

All he thought about
Was that and that!
Hmm…a problem
Silence, her only choice,
But her silence
Only enhanced his thoughts
Of that and that!

Wine and that?
Or
Wine, not that?
Who's to win?
Him or Whim?
This or That?

Poems from an Angel

In a sanctuary of ferns and evergreens,
Protected by shady sentries,
Sunlight peeks though the leaves
Illuminating a Poet's bench.

In solitude, a spirit sits,
infusing the beauty,
all God's gifts.
Magically, she writes.

For all us earthly folks,
She composes a rhyme.
With divine wisdom,
She gives poetry from heaven.

Completing her work, she ascends through the trees.
She leaves behind her inspired verse,
Laying in beams of sun,
Undisturbed on the Poet's bench.

That evening, when her husband returns,
He accepts with great faith
The poems, a celestial gift
From the spirit of his wife.

Beginnings

A school of poetry
Buds promises and possibilities.

New friends awaken
Sleeping potentials.

Today expects
New connections,

Holding a seed
For far-reaching growth.

A sunny day, Autumn colors
Gold, rust, and green

Leaves dance, planes glide
In a cloudless blue.

Our journeys begin
Our paths touch.

Golden days remember
Beginnings.

Flying

I flew today;
it was such fun!

I've been imagining it
for so very long.

I felt myself
up in the sky.

Here I was in Heaven
Flying so high!

Looking down I saw me,
I was just fine.

Returning, I lay
in my bed asleep.

Knowing my dreams
would take me

Again to Heaven
to play and feel so free.

Tender Mercy

Promising poets
welcome me.
October days alight
reddish-gold autumn leaves.
To promote and trust,
We begin a walk of harmony.

Disclosing fears, hopes, dreams
with our quills
our poetry begins to sing.
Like lyrics
we seek accord
until we play a melody.

Through our experiences,
a symbolic touch we make.
Each supplying a note
we emote a symphony.
A rush of feelings
create fellowship in poetry.

Limbo

Oh, gentle star,
Upon whose glow I lay my head,
My tired will to You submit.
My wishes known for You
To grant in time,
That no one fall from grace
Is all I ask.
But such an eternity,
When limbo seems the place I am!
Oh gentle star.

Hymn to God

The soft melodic melodies
In my poems express
The thoughts I wish
To share with you,
Secrets from my heart.
Each day I sit and listen
And pray to be inspired
To hear the things
I need to know
To enlighten me
And diminish my fears.
My pen, as if from dictation,
Takes the message You convey
For me and others
To help along life's way.
But who will hear this message
Apart from me I ask?
Is it my destiny
To deliver the music of poetry?
Of this I know so little
So in Your hands
I place my trust,
And my poems will fall from heaven
Wherever You think they must.

About the Author

I was married in London, and while living there, I began writing poetry. After transferring back to the States, we eventually moved to California, where I was the vice president of the Napa Pen Women, a national organization headquartered in Washington DC. The group consists of writers and composers. I am also a member of a group, the Napa Valley Writers Club, where I read my poetry at wineries and community centers. My poetry is my vocation and my enjoyment.

www.ingramcontent.com/pod-product-compliance
Lightning Source LLC
Chambersburg PA
CBHW020322130626
46549CB00003B/970